YAHOSHUA HA' MASHIAKH KING OF KINGS & HIGH
PRIEST AFTER THE ANCIENT ORDER OF MELCHIZEDEK

יהושע המשיח מלך המלכים וכהן גדול על־סדר
מלכי־צדק הקדמון

WHAT IS THE MAZZAROTH?

In the northern slopes of the Gilboa mountains of Israel, there rests the remains of a sixth century synagogue called Beit Alfa (אלפא בית). This building once housed a congregation of Israelites who kept the commandments of ELOHIM and the faith of YAHOSHUA. After lying dormant for centuries and covered by the sands of time, YAHOWAH in infinite wisdom and foresight allowed this synagogue to be rediscovered and excavated in 1928; followed by a second round of excavation in 1968. Our MASHIAKH said "There is nothing covered, that shall not be revealed; neither hid, that shall not be known." This synagogue has been brought to light in these latter days as a testament and witness to show that not only did the early assemblies of YAHOSHUA keep the law, they also kept the Enoch Calendar.

Assorted on the floor of the Beit Alfa Synagogue are three beautiful excellently preserved mosaics. When you first walk into the synagogue (which has now been turned into a national park and museum), you are greeted with a mosaic depiction of the binding of Isaac by his father, Abraham. On the opposite end of the floor, there is a mosaic of various images including two menorahs, two olive trees, a shofar and several other Hebrew symbols. This section of the synagogue is where the Torah scrolls were housed and read from. In between these two mosaics (which each deserve a writing of their own), there lies an undefined depiction of **the Mazzaroth** (which heathen call Zodiac); which also serves as a calendar based on the measure of time written within the book of Enoch.

The mosaic shows a wheel within a wheel with twelve separate sections in the outer wheel. These twelve sections depict the symbols of the twelve constellations in the Hebrew Mazzaroth. The twelve sections also represent the twelve months within a year. Each section also has the name of their respective constellations. Depicted in the inner wheel is the Glory of YAHOWAH, and four living beasts as described by the prophet Ezekiel, and John the Revelator. On each corner of the outer wheel, there is an Angel.

These Angels are of the Watcher class and are responsible for managing the dividing of the year into four portions (seasons) mentioned in **Enoch 82:11**. "**And these are the names of the leaders who divide the four parts of the year which are ordained: Malkiel (My King is ELOHIM), Elimelek (My ELOHIM is King), and Malʾeyal (I am Filled with ELOHIM), and Nerʾel (Lamp of ELOHIM).**" W...

The 12 Hebrew Mazzaroth

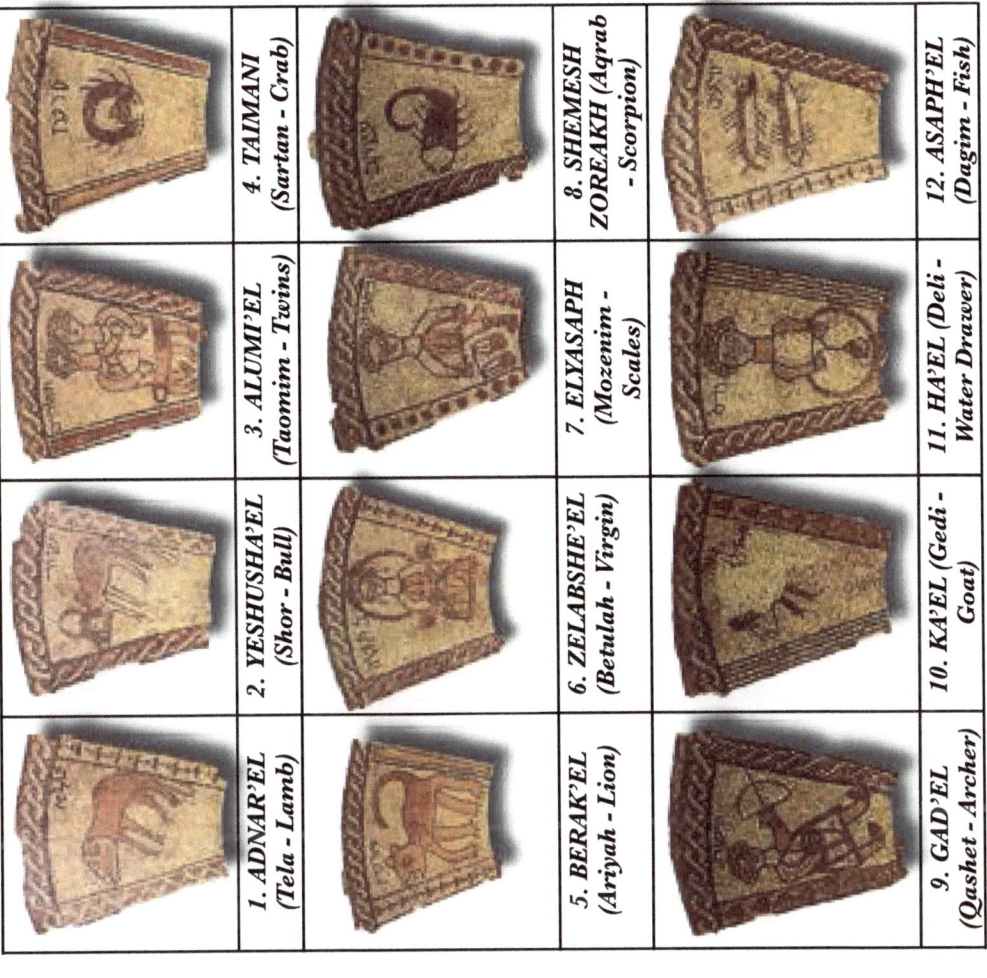

			4. TAIMANI *(Sartan - Crab)*
		3. ALUMI'EL *(Taomim - Twins)*	**8. SHEMESH ZOREAKH** *(Aqrab - Scorpion)*
	2. YESHUSHA'EL *(Shor - Bull)*	**7. ELYASAPH** *(Mozenim - Scales)*	**12. ASAPH'EL** *(Dagim - Fish)*
1. ADNAR'EL *(Tela - Lamb)*	**6. ZELABSHE'EL** *(Betulah - Virgin)*	**11. HA'EL** *(Deli - Water Drawer)*	
	5. BERAK'EL *(Ariyah - Lion)*	**10. KA'EL** *(Gedi - Goat)*	
	9. GAD'EL *(Qashet - Archer)*		

THE BOOK OF ENOCH

The Mosaic does not list the names given to these Angels in the book of Enoch, it does list the portion of the year in which each Angel is responsible for.

Each description starts with the word tĕquwphah (Strong's H8622 תְּקוּפָה) meaning circuit of time or space, and coming around. After this initial word, each Angel then has a month assigned to them which represents the season that they are responsible for. The Angel on the top right has the word "חֶשְׁוָן" next to it which is transliterated as Teshery. This is the Aramaic word for the 7th month of the year. This tells us that this Angel is responsible for the Fall portion of the year. Enoch reveals that this Angel's name is Mali'EL. The Angel on the top left has the word "טֵבֵת" next to it which is Strongs H2887; transliterated as Tebeth and meaning the tenth month. This lets us know that this is the Angel responsible for the Winter portion of the year. Enoch informs us that this Angel's name is Ner'EL. The Angel on the bottom left has the word "נִיסָן" next to it which is Strong's H5212; transliterated as Nisan and meaning the first month of the year. This indicates that this Angel is responsible for the Spring portion of the year. His name listed within the book of Enoch is Malki'EL. Lastly, the Angel on the bottom right corner has the word "תַּמּוּז" which is Strong's H8542; transliterated as Tammuz and meaning the fourth month. This infers that this Angel is responsible for the Summer portion of the year. He is named Elimelek in the book of Enoch.

While much more can be said about this Mosaic image; we can say without doubt that this is assuredly an ancient depiction of the Enoch calendar. This proves that as recent as the sixth century AD, Hebrew believers in **YAHOSHUA** were measuring time based on the writings of the great prophet

Enoch. Daniel, when prophesying of the wicked nations and kings who would arise in the latter days, said that the eleventh horn (king) on the fourth beast (nation) *"shall think to change times and laws."* The Gregorian calendar in which most of the world uses to measure time is a direct fulfilment of this prophecy. This false calendar begins the year during winter where all of nature reflects death and decay.

Enoch's calendar, on the other hand, starts with spring when life is budding and beginning again. It is wiser to measure time in accordance to how the creator of time measures it, rather than following men. **YAHOWAH** is worthy of high praise for revealing these secrets to the saints of the latter days, and for providing us with visual proof and evidence to show that HIS Word is true. Blessed be He who sits upon the throne forever and ever. Amen. *Written by Jonathan Cordero*

Ancient Mazzaroth mosaic at Beit Alfa Synagogue in Heftziba, Israel.

In 2017, a total solar eclipse occurred across North America, where the moon completely blocked the sun, casting a shadow line from the northwest Pacific to the southeast Atlantic and darkening the skies dramatically. In 2024, another solar eclipse will again cross—North America, creating another shadow line from the southwest Pacific to the northeast Atlantic. The intersection of these two shadow lines forms a Taw ת, the last letter of the Hebrew Aleph-Bet. Its value equals 400! Gen 15:13-14

AUGUST 21, 2017 - APRIL 8, 2024
THE SEALING OF THE SAINTS

400 YEARS

YAHOSHUA HA'
MASHIAKH
יהושע המשיח

- 1st Month: Abib
- Symbol: Ram
- Mazzaroth Name: Tela
- Ruling Angel: Adnar'el

TELA = LAMB

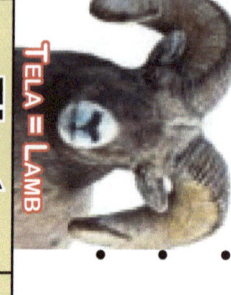

ABIB / אביב
March 2024 5949

The Ram

The first symbol of YAHOSHUA, as the "Lamb slain from the foundation of the world." (Rev 13:8) He is the leader of the sheep, adorned with a crown (horns). This Mazzaroth represents strength, sacrifice and purity.

First Yom Reshon Sunday	Second Yom Shenee Monday	Third Yom Shelishi Tuesday	Fourth Yom Rebi'ee (Midst of Week) Wednesday	Fifth Yom Khamishee Thursday	Sixth Yom Shi'shee Friday	Sabbath Shabbath Saturday
					1 Adar 19	2 Adar 20
3 Adar 21	4 Adar 22	5 Adar 23	6 Adar 24	7 Adar 25	8 Adar 26	9 Adar 27
10 Adar 28	11 Adar 29	12 Adar 30	13 SPRING EQUINOX	14 ABIB 1 New Years Levi's Birth	15 Abib 2	16 Abib 3 GEN 1-4
17 Abib 4	18 Abib 5	19 Abib 6	20 Abib 7	21 Abib 8	22 Abib 9	23 Abib 10 GEN 12-16
24 Abib 11	25 Abib 12	26 Abib 13	27 Crucifixion Passover Eve Abib 14	28 Passover Abib 15	29 Khag Matzah Abib 16	30 Resurrection GEN 17-21 Abib 17
31 Omer 1 Khag Matzah Abib 18						

Enoch The Scribe

חנוך הסופר

IYAR / אייר — April 2024 5949

- 2nd Month: **Iyar**
- Symbol: Bull
- Mazzaroth Name: **Shor**
- Ruling Angel: **Yeshusha'EL**

SHOR = BULL

The Bull symbolizes the leadership and the strength of YAHOSHUA. The Hebrew letter ALEPH is the figure of the Bulls head. The Messiah is the Aleph and Taw. "I am Aleph and Taw, saith YAHOWAH." (REV 1:8)

Sunday Yom Reshon	Monday Yom Shenee	Tuesday Yom Shelishi	Wednesday Yom Rebi'ee (Midst of Week)	Thursday Yom Khamishee	Friday Yom Shi'shee	Sabbath Shabbath
First Yom Reshon	**Second** Yom Shenee	**Third** Yom Shelishi	**Fourth** Yom Rebi'ee (Midst of Week)	**Fifth** Yom Khamishee	**Sixth** Yom Shi'shee	**Sabbath** Shabbath
	1 Omer 2 Khag Matzah Abib 19	**2** Omer 3 Khag Matzah Abib 20	**3** Omer 4 Passover End Abib 21	**4** Omer 5 Abib 22	**5** Martyrdom of James Zebedee	**6** Abib 24 1st Sabbath GEN 22:1-25
7 Omer 8 Abib 25	**8** Alef-Taw Eclipse 400 Years	**9** Omer 10 Abib 27	**10** Omer 11 Abib 28	**11** Omer 12 Abib 29	**12** Omer 13 Abib 30	**13** IYAR 1 Abib 8 2nd Sabbath EXO 12-15
14 Omer 15 Iyar 2	**15** Omer 16 Iyar 3	**16** Omer 17 Iyar 4	**17** Martyrdom of Mark	**18** Omer 19 Iyar 6	**19** Omer 20 Iyar 7	**20** Iyar 8 3rd Sabbath EXO 16-20
21 Omer 22 Iyar 9	**22** Omer 23 Iyar 10	**23** Omer 24 Iyar 11	**24** Omer 25 Iyar 12	**25** Omer 26 Iyar 13	**26** Omer 27 Iyar 14	**27** Iyar 15 Omer 28 EXO 21-25
28 Omer 29 Iyar 16	**29** Omer 30 Iyar 17	**30** Omer 31 Iyar 18				

King & Priest
(Order of Melchizedek)
(מלך וכהן על־סדר מלכי־צדק)

SIWAN / סיון May 2024 5949

- 3rd Month: **Siwan**
- Symbol: **Twins**
- Mazzaroth Name: **Twins**
- Ruling Angel: **Taomim**
- **Alumi'el**

Taomim = Twins
- Symbol: **Taomim**
- Ruling Angel: **Alumi'el**

The Twins

The Twins are symbolic of the two offices that **YAHOSHUA** came to fulfill: **High Priest** & **King of Kings**. The two tribes of **Lewy** and **Yehudah** represent the spirituality and the government of Yisra'el. These two offices become one again when **YAH** establishes the Order of Malki-Tzedeq.

The High Priest and King of Kings

AND WE ALL OF US RAN TOGETHER, AND LEWY LAID HOLD OF THE SUN, AND YEHUDAH OUTSTRIPPED THE OTHERS AND SEIZED THE MOON, AND THEY WERE BOTH OF THEM LIFTED UP WITH THEM, WERE TWELVE RAYS."

First — Yom Reshon — Sunday	Second — Yom Shenee — Monday	Third — Yom Shelishi — Tuesday	Fourth — Yom Rebi'ee (Midst of Week) — Wednesday	Fifth — Yom Khamishee — Thursday	Sixth — Yom Shi'shee — Friday	Sabbath — Shabbath — Saturday
			1 Omer 32 Iyar 19	**2** Omer 33 Iyar 20	**3** Omer 34 Iyar 21	**4** Iyar 22 5th Sabbath Exo 26-30
5 Day of Simon 1 Macc 13:51 Iyar 23	**6** Omer 37 Iyar 24	**7** Omer 38 Iyar 25	**8** Omer 39 Iyar 26	**9** Omer 40 Iyar 27	**10** Omer 41 Iyar 28	**11** Iyar 29 6th Sabbath Exo 31-34
12 Omer 43 Iyar 30	**13** SIWAN 1 Renewed Month	**14** Omer 45 Siwan 2	**15** Omer 46 Siwan 3	**16** Omer 47 Siwan 4	**17** Omer 48 Siwan 5	**18** Siwan 6 7th Sabbath Exo 35-39
19 Shebu'ot Feast of Pentecost (777)	**20** Siwan 8	**21** Siwan 9	**22** Siwan 10	**23** Siwan 11	**24** Martyrdom of Thomas	**25** Siwan 13 Exo 40/Lev 26/Deut 28
26 Siwan 14	**27** Birth of Judah Siwan 15	**28** Siwan 16	**29** Siwan 17	**30** Siwan 18	**31** Siwan 19	

ETHIOPIAN DIASPORA גלות–כושים

- 4th Month: **Tammuz**
- Symbol: **Crab**
- Mazzaroth Name: **Sartan**
- Ruling Angel: **Taimani**

Sartan = Crab

Tammuz / תמוז
June 5949 2024

"Arise, lift up the lad, and hold him in thine hand; for I will make him a great nation." (Genesis 21:18)

He Holds Us In His Hands

Sunday	Monday	Tuesday	Wednesday	Thursday	Friday	Sabbath
First Yom Reshon	**Second** Yom Shenee	**Third** Yom Shelishi	**Fourth** Yom Rebi'ee (Midst of Week)	**Fifth** Yom Khamishee	**Sixth** Yom Shi'shee	**Shabbath** Shabbath
						1 Siwan 20 Deut 1-4
2 Siwan 21	**3** Siwan 22	**4** Siwan 23	**5** Siwan 24	**6** Siwan 25	**7** Siwan 26	**8** Siwan 27 Deut 5-9
9 Siwan 28	**10** Siwan 29	**11** Siwan 30	**12** Summer Solstice	**13** Tammuz 1 Renewed Month Joseph's Birth	**14** Tammuz 2	**15** Tammuz 3 Deut 10-13
16 Tammuz 4	**17** Tammuz 5	**18** Martyrdom of Jude	**19** Martyrdom of Nathaniel	**20** Tammuz 8	**21** Martyrdom of Peter & Paul	**22** Tammuz 10 Deut 14-17
23 Tammuz 11	**24** Tammuz 12	**25** Tammuz 13	**26**	**27** Tammuz 15	**28** Tammuz 16	**29** Tammuz 17 Deut 18-21
30 Tammuz 18						

American Diaspora בלות–אמריקה

- 5th Month: **Ab**
- Symbol: **Lion**
- Mazzaroth
- Name: **Ariyah**
- Ruling Angel: **Berak'el**

ARIYAH = LION

AB / אב
July 5949 2024

The Lion

The Lion is King of all beasts and a fierce protector of his pride. In the same way, **YAHOSHUA** is King of all kings and invincible in battle. Without the male lion, the pride is defenseless and vulnerable.

First Yom Reshon Sunday	Second Yom Shenee Monday	Third Yom Shelishi Tuesday	Fourth Yom Rebi'ee (Midst of Week) Wednesday	Fifth Yom Khamishee Thursday	Sixth Yom Shi'shee Friday	Sabbath Shabbath Saturday
	1 Tammuz 19	2 Tammuz 20	3 Tammuz 21	4 Tammuz 22 Martyrdom of James	5 Tammuz 23	6 Tammuz 24 DEUT 22-25
7 Tammuz 25	8 Tammuz 26	9 Tammuz 27	10 Tammuz 28	11 Tammuz 29	12 Tammuz 30	13 AB 1 Renewed Month DEUT 26-27
14 Ab 2	15 Ab 3	16 Ab 4 Issachar's Birth	17 Ab 5	18 Ab 6	19 Ab 7	20 Ab 8 DEUT 30-34
21 Ab 9	22 Ab 10	23 Ab 11	24 Ab 12	25 Ab 13	26 Ab 14	27 Ab 15 LEV 1-4
28 Ab 16	29 Ab 17	30 Ab 18	31 Ab 19			

The Lion of The Tribe of Judah

AND ONE OF THE ELDERS SAITH UNTO ME, WEEP NOT: BEHOLD, THE LION OF THE TRIBE OF YEHUDAH, THE ROOT OF DAWID, HATH PREVAILED TO OPEN THE BOOK, AND TO LOOSE THE SEVEN SEALS THEREOF. (REVELATION 5:5)

Caribbean Diaspora התפוצות־הקריביות

BETHULAH = VIRGIN

- 6th Month: **Elul**
- Symbol: **Virgin**
- Mazzaroth Name: **Virgin**
- Ruling: **Bethulah**
- Angel: **Zelabshe'el**

ELUL / אלול
August 2024 — 5949

The Virgin represents Miryam YAHOSHUA's mother. Miryam is from the seed of Dawid. She fulfilled the Messianic prophecy given in the Garden of Eden. Miryam's lineage is from Eli (Heli) a descendant of Nathan, son of David in Luke 3:23.

Behold A Virgin Shall Be With Child

"AND IN THE SIXTH MONTH THE ANGEL GABRI'EL WAS SENT... TO A VIRGIN ESPOUSED TO A MAN WHOSE NAME WAS YOSEPH, OF THE HOUSE OF DAWID; AND THE VIRGIN'S NAME WAS MIRYAM.
- LUKE 1:26-28

First Yom Reshon Sunday	Second Yom Shenee Monday	Third Yom Shelishi Tuesday	Fourth Yom Rebi'ee (Midst of Week) Wednesday	Fifth Yom Khamishee Thursday	Sixth Yom Shi'shee Friday	Sabbath Shabbath Saturday
				1 Ab 20	**2** Ab 21	**3** Ab 22 Lev 5-9
4 Ab 23	**5** Ab 24	**6** Ab 25	**7** Ab 26	**8** Ab 27	**9** Ab 28	**10** Ab 29 Lev 10-13
11 Ab 30	**12** Elul 1 — Renewed Month	**13** Elul 2	**14** Elul 3	**15** Elul 4	**16** Elul 5	**17** Elul 6 Lev 14-17
18 Elul 7	**19** Elul 8	**20** Elul 9 — Dan's Birth	**21** Elul 10 — Martyrdom of Bartholomew	**22** Elul 11	**23** Elul 12	**24** Elul 13 Lev 18-21
25 Elul 14	**26** Elul 15	**27** Elul 16	**28** Elul 17	**29** Elul 18	**30** Elul 19	**31** Elul 20 Lev 22-25/27

Ghanian Diaspora בית־כנסת

TISHREI / תשרי
September 5949/2024

The Scales

The Hebrew word for scales is the same word for balances. Scales were used to measure out the cost to pay for something. YAHOSHUA used His own blood and weighed it in the balance to pay for all of our sins.

- 7th Month: **Tishrei**
- Symbol: **Scales**
- Mazzaroth Name: **Mozenim**
- Ruling Angel: **El'yasaph**

MOZENIM = SCALES

First Yom Reshon Sunday	Second Yom Shenee Monday	Third Yom Shelishi Tuesday	Fourth Yom Rebi'ee (Midst of Week) Wednesday	Fifth Yom Khamishee Thursday	Sixth Yom Shi'shee Friday	Sabbath Shabbath Saturday
1 Elul 21	**2** Elul 22	**3** Elul 23	**4** Elul 24	**5** Elul 25	**6** Elul 26	**7** Elul 27 EXO 1-4
8 Elul 28	**9** Elul 29	**10** Elul 30	**11** FALL EQUINOX	**12** TISHREI 1 Yom Teruah	**13** Tishrei 2	**14** Tishrei 3 EXO 5-8
15 Tishrei 4	**16** Naphtali's Birth Tishrei 5	**17** Tishrei 6	**18** Zebulon's Birth Tishrei 7	**19** Tishrei 8	**20** Tishrei 9	**21** Yom Kippur EXO 9-11
22 Tishrei 11	**23** Tishrei 12	**24** Tishrei 13	**25** Sukkoth Eve Tishrei 14	**26** Sukkoth Tishrei 15	**27** Tishrei 16	**28** Tishrei 17 GEN 5-8
29 Tishrei 18	**30** Tishrei 19					

"LET ME BE WEIGHED IN AN EVEN BALANCE, THAT ELOHIM MAY KNOW MINE INTEGRITY." (JOB 31:6) "WHO HATH MEASURED THE WATERS IN THE HOLLOW OF HIS HAND, AND METED OUT HEAVEN WITH THE SPAN, AND COMPREHENDED THE DUST OF THE EARTH IN A MEASURE, AND WEIGHED THE MOUNTAINS IN SCALES, AND THE HILLS IN A BALANCE?" (ISA 40:12)

Jerusalem Diaspora ישראלים–הגלות

Kheswan / חשון — October 2024 — 5949

8th Month: Kheshwan
Symbol: Scorpion
Mazzaroth Name: Scorpion
Ruling Angel: Shemesh Zoreakh

Aqrab = Kheshwan
Scorpion: Kheshwan
Aqrab

The Scorpion

YAHOSHUA's victory over death is represented by Him crushing the head of the Scorpion. When His foot trode upon the Scorpion's head, its tail stung YAHOSHUA's heel. He had to endure death to defeat the Devil.

First — Yom Reshon — Sunday	Second — Yom Shenee — Monday	Third — Yom Shelishi — Tuesday	Fourth — Yom Rebi'ee (Midst of Week) — Wednesday	Fifth — Yom Khamishee — Thursday	Sixth — Yom Shi'shee — Friday	Sabbath — Shabbath — Saturday
		1 Martyrdom of Matthew	**2** Tishrei 21	**3** End Sukkoth Tishrei 22	**4** Tishrei 23	**5** Tishrei 24 GEN 9–11
6 Tishrei 25	**7** Tishrei 26	**8** Tishrei 27	**9** Tishrei 28	**10** Tishrei 29	**11** Martyrdom of Luke	**12** KHESHWAN 1 Renewed Month NUM 1–3
13 Kheshwan 2	**14** Kheshwan 3	**15** Kheshwan 4	**16** Kheshwan 5	**17** Kheshwan 6	**18** Kheshwan 7	**19** Kheshwan 8 GEN 49–50
20 Kheshwan 9	**21** Kheshwan 10	**22** Benjamini's Birth Kheshwan 11	**23** Gad's Birth Kheshwan 12	**24** Kheshwan 13	**25** Kheshwan 14	**26** Kheshwan 15 GEN 26–29
27 Kheshwan 16	**28** Kheshwan 17	**29** Kheshwan 18	**30** Kheshwan 19	**31** Kheshwan 20		

"AND HE SAID UNTO THEM, I BEHELD SATAN AS LIGHTNING FALL FROM HEAVEN. BEHOLD, I GIVE UNTO YOU POWER TO TREAD ON SERPENTS AND SCORPIONS, AND OVER ALL THE POWER OF THE ENEMY: AND NOTHING SHALL BY ANY MEANS HURT YOU." - LUKE 10:18

IGBO DIASPORA אִיגְבּוֹ-אָזוֹר

KISLEW / כסלו
November 5949 2024

- 9th Month: **Kislew**
- Symbol: **Archer**
- Mazzaroth Name: **Qashet**
- Ruling Angel: **Gad'El**

QASHET = ARCHER

The Archer

The Archer depicts **YAHOSHUA**, as victorious over death. He holds the bow and arrows in His hands. In the book of Revelation **YAHOSHUA** leads the 144,000 and the Heavenly Host into victory over the Dragon and the Beast.

"YEA, HE SENT OUT HIS ARROWS, AND SCATTERED THEM; AND HE SHOT OUT LIGHTNINGS, AND DISCOMFITED THEM."
PSALMS 21:12

The Arrows of Yahoshua

First Yom Reshon Sunday	Second Yom Shenee Monday	Third Yom Shelishi Tuesday	Fourth Yom Rebi'ee (Midst of Week) Wednesday	Fifth Yom Khamishee Thursday	Sixth Yom Shi'shee Friday	Sabbath Shabbath Saturday
					1 Kheshwan 21	**2** Kheshwan 22 GEN 30-33
3 Kheshwan 23	**4** Kheshwan 24	**5** Kheshwan 25	**6** Kheshwan 26 Martyrdom of Philip	**7** Kheshwan 27	**8** Kheshwan 28	**9** Kheshwan 29 NUM 4-7
10 Kheshwan 30	**11** KISLEW 1 Renewed Month	**12** Kislew 2	**13** Kislew 3	**14** Kislew 4	**15** Kislew 5	**16** Kislew 6 NUM 8-11
17 Kislew 7	**18** Kislew 8	**19** Kislew 9	**20** Kislew 10	**21** Kislew 11	**22** Kislew 12 Martyrdom of Andrew	**23** Kislew 13 GEN 34-37
24 Reuben's Birth Kislew 14	**25** Kislew 15	**26** Kislew 16	**27** Kislew 17	**28** Kislew 18	**29** Kislew 19	**30** Kislew 20 GEN 38-41

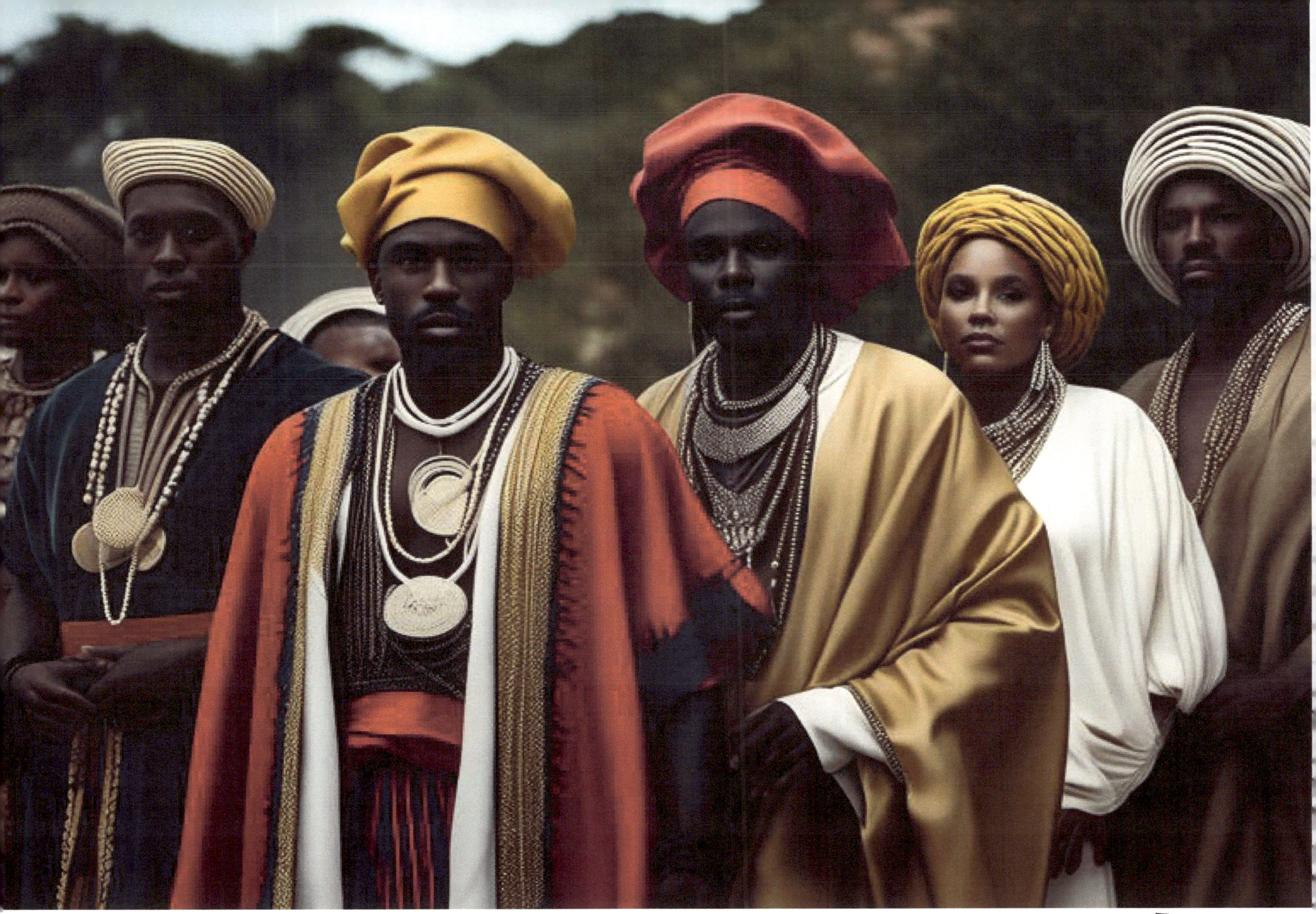

South African Diaspora גלות-דרום אפריקה

GEDI = GOAT

- 10th Month: **Tebet**
- Symbol: **Tebet**
- Mazzaroth Name: **Goat**
- Ruling Angel: **Gedi**
- **Ka'EL**

TEBET / טבת
December
5949   2024

The Goat

After **YAHOSHUA's** confrontation with the Scorpion and subsequent death and resurrection, His precious blood became the Sin Offering for our souls. The goat is the animal that is sacrificed on Yom Kippur for the sins of Yisra'EL.

First Yom Reshon Sunday	Second Yom Shenee Monday	Third Yom Shelishi Tuesday	Fourth Yom Rebi'ee (Midst of Week) Wednesday	Fifth Yom Khamishee Thursday	Sixth Yom Shi'shee Friday	Sabbath Shabbath Saturday
1 Kislew 21	**2** Kislew 22	**3** Kislew 23	**4** Khanukah Eve Kislew 24	**5** Khanukah Kislew 25	**6** Kislew 26	**7** Kislew 27 NUM 12–15
8 Kislew 28	**9** Kislew 29	**10** Kislew 30	**11** WINTER SOLSTICE	**12** TEBET 1 End Khanukah	**13** Tebet 2	**14** Tebet 3 NUM 16–19
15 Tebet 4	**16** Tebet 5	**17** Tebet 6	**18** Tebet 7	**19** Tebet 8	**20** Tebet 9	**21** Tebet 10 GEN 42–45
22 Ascension of John	**23** Tebet 12	**24** Tebet 13	**25** Tebet 14	**26** Tebet 15	**27** Tebet 16	**28** Tebet 17 GEN 46–48
29 Tebet 18	**30** Tebet 19	**31** Tebet 20				

The Sin Offering

"Then shall he kill the goat of the sin offering, that is for the people, and bring his blood within the vail... and sprinkle it upon the mercy seat." -
Leviticus 16:15

English Diaspora אנגלית–גלות

SHEBAT / שבט

January 5949 2025

First Yom Reshon Sunday	Second Yom Shenee Monday	Third Yom Shelishi Tuesday	Fourth Yom Rebi'ee (Midst of Week) Wednesday	Fifth Yom Khamishee Thursday	Sixth Yom Shi'shee Friday	Sabbath Shabbath Shabbath

11th Month: Shebat
Symbol: Water Drawer
Mazzaroth Name: Aqrab
Ruling Angel: Ha'El

DEU 11 : 11th Month: Shebat
WATER : Symbol: Water Drawer
DRAWER : Mazzaroth Name: Aqrab
Ruling Angel: Ha'El

__The Water Bearer__

When YAHOSHUA was crucified, His side was pierced and blood and water flowed out. His blood was the outpouring of THE RUAKH HA' QODESH (The Holy Spirit). The Water Bearer pours out His RUAKH into His Disciples.

__The Pitcher of Water__

"AND HE SENDETH FORTH TWO OF HIS DISCIPLES, AND SAITH UNTO THEM, GO YE INTO THE CITY, AND THERE SHALL MEET YOU A MAN BEARING A PITCHER OF WATER: FOLLOW HIM." (MARK 14:13)

			1 Simeon's Birth Tebet 21	**2** Tebet 22	**3** Tebet 23	**4** Tebet 24 NUM 20-23
5 Tebet 25	**6** Tebet 26	**7** Tebet 27	**8** Tebet 28	**9** Tebet 29	**10** Tebet 30	**11** SHEBAT 1 Renewed Month NUM 24-27
12 Asher's Birth Shebat 2	**13** Shebat 3	**14** Shebat 4	**15** Shebat 5	**16** Shebat 6	**17** Shebat 7	**18** Shebat 8 NUM 28-31
19 Shebat 9	**20** Shebat 10	**21** Shebat 11	**22** Shebat 12	**23** Shebat 13	**24** Shebat 14	**25** Shebat 15 NUM 32-33
26 Shebat 16	**27** Martyrdom of James Alpheus	**28** Shebat 18	**29** Shebat 19	**30** Shebat 20	**31** Shebat 21	

Indian Diaspora גלות-הודו

ADAR / אדר 5949 February 2025

- **12th Month:** Adar
- **Symbol:** Fish
- **Mazzaroth**
- **Name:** Dagim
- **Ruling Angel:** Asaph'EL

DAGIM = FISH

The Fish

Since YAHOSHUA poured out His RUAKH which is represented by water, then we like fish must be able to live in that water. True Disciples live in the Spirit as fish live in the water. It is our job to become fishers of men.

"YAHOSHUA SAITH UNTO THEM, BRING OF THE FISH WHICH YE HAVE NOW CAUGHT. SHIMON KEPHA WENT UP, AND DREW THE NET TO LAND FULL OF GREAT FISHES." (JOHN 21:10-11)

The Fishers Net

"And YAHOSHUA said unto them, Come ye after me, and I will make you to become fishers of men." Mark 1:17

Fishers of Men

First — Yom Reshon — Sunday	Second — Yom Shenee — Monday	Third — Yom Shelishi — Tuesday	Fourth — Yom Rebi'ee (Midst of Week) — Wednesday	Fifth — Yom Khamishee — Thursday	Sixth — Yom Shi'shee — Friday	Sabbath — Shabbath — Saturday
						1 Shebat 22 NUM 34-36
2 Shebat 23	**3** Shebat 24	**4** Shebat 25	**5** Shebat 26	**6** Shebat 27	**7** Shebat 28	**8** Shebat 29 EXO 12
9 Shebat 30	**10** ADAR 1 Renewed Month	**11** Adar 2	**12** Adar 3	**13** Adar 4	**14** Adar 5	**15** Adar 6
16 Adar 7	**17** Adar 8	**18** Adar 9	**19** Adar 10	**20** Adar 11	**21** Adar 12	**22** Adar 13
23 1st Day Purim Apostle of Yahoshua	**24** 2nd Day Purim Adar 15	**25** Adar 16	**26** Adar 17	**27** Adar 18	**28** Adar 19	

Bantu Diaspora בֶּנְטוּ־גוֹלוּת

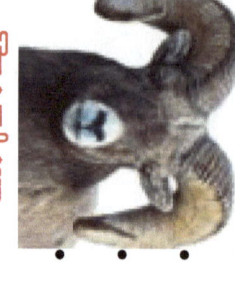

ABIB / אביב

March 5950 2025

TELA = LAMB

- 1st Month: Abib
- Symbol: Abib
- Mazzaroth Symbol: Ram
- Name: Tela
- Ruling Angel: Adnar'El

The Ram

The first symbol of YAHOSHUA, as the "Lamb slain from the foundation of the world." (Rev 13:8) He is the leader of the sheep, adorned with a crown (horns). This Mazzaroth represents strength, sacrifice and purity.

First Yom Reshon Sunday	Second Yom Shenee Monday	Third Yom Shelishi Tuesday	Fourth Yom Rebi'ee (Midst of Week) Wednesday	Fifth Yom Khamishee Thursday	Sixth Yom Shi'shee Friday	Sabbath Shabbath Saturday
						1 Adar 20
2 Adar 21	3 Adar 22	4 Adar 23	5 Adar 24	6 Adar 25	7 Adar 26	8 Adar 27
9 Adar 28	10 Adar 29	11 Adar 30	12 Spring Equinox	13 ABIB 1 New Years Levi's Birth	14 Abib 2	15 Abib 3
16 Abib 4	17 Abib 5	18 Abib 6	19 Abib 7	20 Abib 8	21 Abib 9	22 Abib 10
23 Abib 11	24 Abib 12	25 Abib 13	26 Crucifixion Passover Eve Abib 14	27 Passover Abib 15	28 Khag Matzah Abib 16	29 YAHOSHUA's Resurrection Abib 17
30 Omer 1 Khag Matzah Abib 18	31 Omer 2 Khag Matzah Abib 19					

Order of Melchizedek זכריה מלכי-צדק

- 2nd Month: Iyar
- Symbol: Bull
- Name: Mazzaroth
- Ruling Shor
- Angel: Yeshusha'EL

The Bull symbolizes the leadership and the strength of YAHOSHUA. The Hebrew letter ALEPH is the figure of the Bulls head. The Messiah is the Aleph and Taw. "I am Aleph and Taw, saith YAHOWAH." (Rev 1:8)

First Yom Reshon Sunday	Second Yom Shenee Monday	Third Yom Shelishi Tuesday	Fourth Yom Rebi'ee (Midst of Week) Wednesday	Fifth Yom Khamishee Thursday	Sixth Yom Shi'shee Friday	Sabbath Shabbath Saturday
		1 Omer 3 Khag Matzah Abib 20	**2** Omer 4 Passover End Abib 21	**3** Omer 5 Abib 22	**4** Martyrdom of James Zebedee	**5** 1st Sabbath Abib 24
6 Omer 8 Abib 25	**7** Omer 9 Abib 26	**8** Omer 10 Abib 27	**9** Omer 11 Abib 28	**10** Omer 12 Abib 29	**11** Omer 13 Abib 30	**12** IYAR 1 2nd Sabbath
13 Omer 15 Iyar 2	**14** Omer 16 Iyar 3	**15** Omer 17 Iyar 4	**16** Martyrdom of Mark	**17** Omer 19 Iyar 6	**18** Omer 20 Iyar 7	**19** 3rd Sabbath Iyar 8
20 Omer 22 Iyar 9	**21** Omer 23 Iyar 10	**22** Omer 24 Iyar 11	**23** Omer 25 Iyar 12	**24** Omer 26 Iyar 13	**25** Omer 27 Iyar 14	**26** Omer 28 Iyar 15
27 Omer 29 Iyar 16	**28** Omer 30 Iyar 17	**29** Omer 31 Iyar 18	**30** Omer 32 Iyar 19			

The Firstborn Birthright and The Bull

"AND LO, A BULL UPON THE EARTH, WITH TWO GREAT HORNS, AND AN EAGLE'S WINGS UPON HIS BACK; AND WE WISHED TO SEIZE HIM, BUT COULD NOT. BUT YOSEPH CAME, AND SEIZED HIM, AND ASCENDED UP WITH HIM ON HIGH." (NAPHTALI 5:6-7)